Spirit

IN NATURE

Spirit
IN NATURE

Teaching Judaism and Ecology
on the Trail

MATT BIERS-ARIEL

DEBORAH NEWBRUN

MICHAL FOX SMART

It is with great appreciation for his books *Sharing Nature with Children* (the original outdoor teaching activity guide) and *Sharing the Joy of Nature* (both published by Dawn Publications, Nevada City, CA,) that we acknowledge the ideas and activities of our teacher Joseph Cornell. The following activities in *Spirit in Nature* were adapted from these works as follows:

"Opening the Eyes of the Blind"
   "Camera" (*Sharing the Joy of Nature*)
"Sh'ma: Listen"
   "Sounds" (*Sharing Nature with Children*)
"Bal Tash'hit and the Great Garbage Hunt"
   "Unnature Trail" (*Sharing Nature with Children*)
"Build a Tree of Life"
   "Build a Tree" (*Sharing the Joy of Nature*)
"Bringing On the Night"
   "Caterpillar Walk," "Bat and Moth" (*Sharing Nature with Children*)

"T'filat Haderech" from AND YOU SHALL BE A BLESSING,
music by Debbie Friedman, lyrics by Debbie Friedman
(based on traditional text); © 1988 Deborah Lynn Friedman (ASCAP);
Sounds Write Productions, Inc. (ASCAP).

This book is printed on recycled paper.
MANUFACTURED IN THE UNITED STATES OF AMERICA

Library of Congress Cataloging-in-Publication Data

Biers-Ariel, Matt.
   Spirit in nature : teaching Judaism and ecology on the trail / by Matt Biers-Ariel,
   Deborah Newbrun, Michal Fox Smart.
      p. cm.
   ISBN 13: 978-0-87441-686-2 (trade pbk.)
   ISBN 10:   0-87441-686-8 (trade pbk.)

   1. Human ecology--Religious aspects--Judaism. 2. Nature--Religious aspects--Judaism.
3. Hiking for children--Planning. I. Newbrun, Deborah. II Smart, Michal Fox. III Title.

BM538.H85 B54 2000

ૐ

TABLE OF CONTENTS

FOREWORD

Trees, gardens, plants, and orchards play a significant role in traditional Jewish literature. Beginning with the biblical story of the Garden of Eden and progressing through the rabbinic period, an awareness of the complexity of the human relationship to the natural environment has figured prominently in Judaism's literary and legal landscapes.

Take, for example, our primal story. That narrative, documenting the first human search for knowledge, makes clear that from the beginning we have been tied organically to nature and its God-given secrets. The link to the Garden of Eden and its message of our bond with the natural world is reflected even in the rabbinic term for the overarching concepts of all textual exegesis—*pardes*. While *pardes* is an acronym formed from the four traditional modes of interpreting texts, it is also the Hebrew word for orchard and for paradise. And so *pardes*, the orchard, represents the repository of eternal truth and wisdom.

Acquiring the fruits of the orchard of wisdom does not come easily, yet these fruits can be accessible to all of us; they are ours to pursue. If we carry out our quest with vigor and always with considerable care, new worlds are created and revealed. The *pardes* in which we search is no longer an environmental locus of being, a particular place that defines us, but an analogue to the entire world—and to the mysteries of the universe.

And so we compare our Torah, our source of truth, to the tree—and to tap the truths of the tree, it must be seen, heard, and felt. The Talmud records the statement that Rabbi Yohanan understood the language of trees. We, in the 21st century, need to emulate Rabbi Yohanan's skill.

In *Spirit in Nature*, you will find resources that will enable you to reach the Truth through a combination of understanding our environment and our sacred texts. In creating their mix of activities, the authors never lost sight of our hallowed tradition. Matt Biers-Ariel, Deborah Newbrun, and Michal Fox Smart are to be commended for having jostled our potential for awareness—of ourselves, our universe, and our tradition.

May this guide become well-worn. May other such guides be written and used. And may you, the reader, have an intense journey, marked by new links and learnings, so that you, too, can come to understand the language of the trees.

—Stuart L. Kelman
Rabbi, Congregation Netivot Shalom
Berkeley, California
Purim 5760

ACKNOWLEDGMENTS

With thanks and love I acknowledge two great Jewish teachers and friends: Rabbi Stuart Kelman and singer/songwriter Debbie Friedman. The work I did with them during the M'ayan *tefilah* teacher retreats caused me to think about connecting Judaism and ecology and was the stage on which I developed many of these activities. Thanks also to my friends at Exploring New Horizons: Laura Tucker, Don Klienfelder, Steve Van Zant, Mark Nolan, Bob Flasher, and Kim Woodland; with them I first entered the out-of-doors as an educator and began to teach children how to love the earth. My colleagues and companions at Camp Tawonga—Ken Kramarz and Ann Gonski—encourage my creativity as a Jewish educator and provide lots of teaching opportunities at our wonderful children's Jewish summer camp near Yosemite. Most important, thanks to my parents, Erni and Eva Newbrun, who took me outside as a little girl and taught me to love nature's splendor. Finally, I offer an expression of love and thanks to my *beshert*, Rabbi Sydney Mintz, who teaches, supports, and loves me every day.

—Deborah Newbrun

As I wrote this book, many people lent me support; I would like to thank the Coalition on the Environment and Jewish Life for supporting this book in its beginnings; my children, Zach and Jonah, for their patience as this project was completed; my parents, David and Louise Fox and Robert and Martha Smart, for providing child care and encouragement; James for walking with me through this world and sharing the wonder; and the *Kadosh Baruch Hu* for the gift of life.

—Michal Fox Smart

Thanks to the naturalists of the Venture West School of Outdoor Living (circa 1983), who sparked my fire and taught me how to teach.

—Matt Biers-Ariel

INTRODUCTION

Judaism's roots are in nature. It was in the wilderness that Jacob dreamed of a ladder reaching to heaven, Moses spoke with God at the burning bush, and the children of Israel received the Torah. The people of the Bible were a people of the land. Our stories, laws, and sacred writings reflect the environmental wisdom of our people. Today many of us live in urban centers or suburbs and have lost our connection to the natural world. The biosphere that nurtures us suffers from overpopulation, unbridled consumerism, extensive pollution, massive extinction, and habitat destruction. In a time when many Jews are searching for a path to spiritual growth, the land beckons us to return. Judaism offers us ways of interacting with the environment that are both nurturing and sustaining.

In Genesis 13:17 God commands Abraham, "Walk about the land [of Canaan], through its length and its breadth, for I give it to you." This biblical narrative implies that Abraham could not encounter the Promised Land abstractly. Rather, he had to walk the land—climb its slopes, cross its streams, feel its heat, encounter its flora and fauna, and protect himself from its dangers to forge a covenant with it. The Bible suggests that a people can merit the inheritance of a land only through the intimate, living experience of it. This is true not only for those who live in Israel, but for all people living on earth.

You need not be a naturalist to benefit from this book. The only requirement is a willingness to venture outdoors with open eyes. Bring this book as a companion on the trail; its activities, texts, stories, and blessings will help you discover and experience the beauty of God's creation and the wisdom of the Jewish tradition in interacting with it. The activities can be done singly or can be combined and may be adapted for groups of all ages and physical abilities.

We hope that using this book will leave you and your companion hikers with a deepened sense of caring for special places you visit and for the environment as a whole. Spending time in natural settings leads to a better understanding of our role in the natural world. When this happens, we will truly be able to fulfill the mitzvah of *tikkun olam*—repairing the world.

If the pages of this book become dog-eared, smudged with mud, torn, and graced with pen markings, that will be the surest sign that you are putting it to the best use. Now go get dirty!

Spirit

IN NATURE

CHAPTER 1

Beginnings, Endings, Group Building

---

successful nature hike is not just a walk in the woods. Much like a meal that begins and ends with a blessing, or like the Torah, which is blessed before and after it is read, a nature hike, properly begun and ended, can become a spiritual journey.

A well-planned beginning can create sacred time and space for hikers to enter. It is within this space and time that hikers may encounter the miracles and magic of creation. A meaningful ending to a nature walk enables hikers to take their experiences and lessons with them long after they wash the mud from their boots.

Building community can be one of the most valuable experiences on a hike. A group joined in spiritual awareness can often discover more in the woods or a field—and feel it more deeply—than the solitary wanderer can. Observing a beautiful sunset as a group strengthens a community by giving participants a shared spiritual experience. Even overcoming obstacles encountered on the trail brings hikers closer together as they learn to help and depend on one another.

Experiencing meaningful beginnings and endings, creating spiritual moments, and building a community happen only with intention. The activities in this section suggest some beginnings and endings that can help to turn an ordinary walk in the woods into a journey of the spirit.

T'filat Haderech: Traveler's Prayer

'filat Haderech, the traveler's prayer (literally, "prayer of the road"), beseeches God to protect travelers from the dangers faced on a journey. While today the most dangerous part of almost every hike is the transportation in automobiles to and from the trail head, reciting T'filat Haderech is a wonderful way to launch a hike as a journey into God's creation.

Ages: 10+

Hikers' Goals:

- to be familiar with T'filat Haderech

- to look forward to the beginning of the journey

- to share everyone's fears and hopes about the hike

Procedure:

Gather the group at the trailhead and recite T'filat Haderech together. Choose either one of the two versions provided, write your own, or have the group create its own. Make copies for everyone in your group, or pass the blessing around so that each hiker can read one line. Explain that reciting this prayer is a way to help focus the hikers' goals, hopes, and fears about their impending walk.

If this is the first wilderness trip for group members or if it is their first hike of the year, reciting the Sheheḥeyanu blessing may be appropriate. The Sheheḥeyanu, a prayer recited on joyous occasions or when we do something for the first time, expresses thanks to God for allowing us to reach this special moment.

T'filat Haderech (traditional text)

יְהִי רָצוֹן מִלְּפָנֶיךָ יְיָ אֱלֹהֵינוּ וֵאלֹהֵי אֲבוֹתֵינוּ, שֶׁתּוֹלִיכֵנוּ לְשָׁלוֹם
וְתַצְעִידֵנוּ לְשָׁלוֹם וְתִסְמְכֵנוּ לְשָׁלוֹם, וְתַגִּיעֵנוּ לִמְחוֹז חֶפְצֵנוּ
לְחַיִּים וּלְשִׂמְחָה וּלְשָׁלוֹם, וְתַחֲזִירֵנוּ לְבֵיתֵנוּ לְשָׁלוֹם. וְתַצִּילֵנוּ
מִכַּף כָּל־אוֹיֵב וְאוֹרֵב וְאָסוֹן בַּדֶּרֶךְ וּמִכָּל־מִינֵי פֻּרְעָנִיּוֹת
הַמִּתְרַגְּשׁוֹת לָבוֹא לָעוֹלָם. וְתִשְׁלַח בְּרָכָה בְּמַעֲשֵׂה יָדֵינוּ, וְתִתְּנֵנוּ
לְחֵן וּלְחֶסֶד וּלְרַחֲמִים בְּעֵינֶיךָ וּבְעֵינֵי כָל־רוֹאֵינוּ. וְתִשְׁמַע קוֹל
תַּחֲנוּנֵינוּ, כִּי אֵל שׁוֹמֵעַ תְּפִלָּה וְתַחֲנוּן אָתָּה. בָּרוּךְ אַתָּה יְיָ
שׁוֹמֵעַ תְּפִלָּה.

Y'hi ratzon mi'l'fanecha, Adonai Eloheinu veilohei avoteinu, shetolicheinu l'shalom v'tatzideinu l'shalom v'tasm'cheinu l'shalom, v'tagi'einu lim'hoz ḥeftzeinu l'ḥayyim ul'simḥah ul'shalom, v'taḥazireinu l'veiteinu l'shalom. V'hatzileinu mikaf kol-oyeiv v'oreiv v'ason baderech umikol-minei pur'aniyot hamitragshot lavo la'olam. V'tishlaḥ brachah b'ma'aseh yadeinu, v'titneinu l'ḥen ul'ḥesed ul'raḥamim b'einecha uveinei chol ro'einu. V'tishma kol taḥanuneinu, ki eil shomei'a t'filah v'taḥanun atah. Baruch atah Adonai shomei'a t'filah.

May it be your will, Adonai, our God and God of our ancestors, to lead us in peace, to keep us in peace, to direct us to our destination in health and happiness and peace, and to return us to our homes in peace. Save us from all enemies and calamities on the journey, and from all threatening disasters. Bless the work of our hands. May we find grace, love, and mercy in your sight and in the sight of all who see us. Hear our pleas, for You listen to prayer and supplication. Praised are You, Adonai, who hears prayer.

T'filat Haderech (contemporary version)

May we be blessed as we go on our way,
May we be guided in peace,
May we be blessed with health and joy,
May this be our blessing Amen.
May we be sheltered by the wings of peace,
May we be kept in safety and in love,
May grace and compassion find their way to every soul,
May this be our blessing Amen.
   —FROM *And You Shall Be a Blessing*
   BY DEBBIE FRIEDMAN

Sheheḥeyanu

בָּרוּךְ אַתָּה, יְיָ אֱלֹהֵינוּ, מֶלֶךְ הָעוֹלָם, שֶׁהֶחֱיָנוּ וְקִיְּמָנוּ וְהִגִּיעָנוּ לַזְּמַן הַזֶּה.

Baruch atah, Adonai Eloheinu, Melech ha'olam, sheheḥeyanu v'kiyemanu v'higiyanu lazman hazeh.

Blessed are You, Adonai our God, Ruler of the universe, who has kept us alive and sustained us and brought us to this time.

Questions to Ask Hikers:

• What do you hope to learn on this hike?

• The blessing asks God to "save us from every enemy and disaster along the way." What do you fear on this journey?

• T'filat Haderech says, "Bless the work of our hands." How can our actions bring blessing to the world—to specific places, creatures, or people we encounter?

- What is the connection between asking God to "bless the work of our hands" and our responsibility to do *tikkun olam* (repairing the world) on every journey we take?

Moses' Staff

hen God charged Moses to lead the children of Israel out of Egypt, he initially declined, saying that the Israelites would not believe he had been chosen by God. So to convince the Israelites of Moses' authenticity, God endowed his staff with magical powers. Not only did the staff prove to be a useful tool for Moses, but it also served to remind him of God's presence in his life.

At various times during the hike, you may want to stop and have hikers share their thoughts and feelings. Some might have difficulty in expressing themselves, however, and a ritual object can help focus hikers' attention and ease discussion, in much the same way that the "magic" staff helped Moses.

Ages: 8+

Hikers' Goals:

- to feel comfortable sharing thoughts and feelings
- to develop active listening skills

Time:

- at the end of an individual experience, such as a "lone sit" or "lone walk"
- during a night hike
- during a concluding ritual
- when dealing with a difficult group issue

Materials:

- a wooden stick or some other object
  (for example, a large crystal or a feather)

Procedure:

Have hikers sit in a circle. Explain the ground rules for using Moses' staff (see below). The staff is then either passed around the circle or the one holding the staff gives it to another person who has signaled for it. It may be a good idea for the leader to begin and to set the proper tone.

Suggested Ground Rules:

- Only the person holding Moses' staff may talk.

- All others must listen.

- Everyone has the right to decline the opportunity to talk.

- All hikers must show respect for the speaker's feelings.

- Hikers must agree not to repeat what they've heard to anyone outside the group.

- Participants should try not to repeat what has already been said.

Modim Anaḥnu Lach: Giving Thanks

A concluding passage in the Amidah prayer thanks God for the gift of living in this wondrous world. The liturgy reads as follows: "We thank You, God . . . for our lives, which depend upon your hand . . . and for your miracles and your goodness, which are with us in every moment: evening, morning, and noon."

This activity supplements the traditional prayer of thanksgiving. It is a religious way of "debriefing" after a wilderness

---

experience and bringing closure to the end of a hike or extended trip.

Ages: 7+

Hikers' Goals:

• to express thanks at the conclusion of a nature experience

Procedure:

Explain that as a group the hikers will be thanking God through prayer for all of the good things they experienced during the hike. Allow the group members a few moments of silent reflection to recall the terrain and their experiences along the way. For an extended trip it may be helpful to review the trip's starting point, the major activities, and the most notable sites along the way. Each person may speak whenever moved to do so. The group facilitator should begin the collective prayer by reciting aloud:

מוֹדִים אֲנַחְנוּ לָךְ, שָׁאַתָּה הוּא יְיָ אֱלֹהֵינוּ וֵאלֹהֵי אֲבוֹתֵינוּ
(וְאִמּוֹתֵינוּ)...

"Modim anaḥnu lach, sha'atah hu Adonai Eloheinu v'elohei avoteinu v'imoteinu..."

"We thank you, Adonai, our God, and God of our fathers (and mothers) for . . ."

Hikers now complete this collective prayer as thoughts come to mind—perhaps something they experienced on the hike for which they want to give thanks. Descriptive words or phrases work best—for example, "chirping birds," "dry socks," "helping hands," or "rain that makes my shoes squeak." It may be helpful for the leader to start by offering a phrase or having someone else ready to begin. Be comfortable with moments of silence as hikers gather their thoughts.

When you sense the momentum has slowed and it is time
to close, add the concluding words of the traditional prayer:

עַל חַיֵּינוּ הַמְּסוּרִים בְּיָדֶךְ וְעַל נִשְׁמוֹתֵינוּ הַפְּקוּדוֹת לָךְ וְעַל נִסֶּיךָ
שֶׁבְּכָל-יוֹם עִמָּנוּ וְעַל נִפְלְאוֹתֶיךָ וְטוֹבוֹתֶיךָ שֶׁבְּכָל-עֵת, עֶרֶב וָבֹקֶר
וְצָהֳרָיִם.

"...al ḥayeinu ha'm'surim b'yadecha v'al nishmoteinu ha'p'kudot lach v'al
nisecha sheb'chol-yom imanu v'al niflotecha v'tovotecha sheb'chol-et, erev
vavoker v'tzohorayim."

"...and for our lives, which depend upon your hand, and for
your miracles and your goodness, which are with us at every
moment: evening, morning, and noon."

CHAPTER 2

Opening Our Eyes to Miracles

oses first encountered God while shepherding his flock in the wilderness surrounding Mount Horeb. An angel of God appeared to him in a flame of fire from within a bush. As Moses gazed at the bush, he saw it was not being consumed by the flame. It was then that God called to Moses.

Jews have struggled throughout history to interpret this miracle. Here is one interpretation: The shepherd Moses was a keen observer of his environment—he had to be in order to spot dangerous animals and find pastures for grazing and water sources. One day he was gazing at an ordinary bush. The longer he looked, the more intrigued he became with this plant. After watching for a long time, Moses began to see the bush's life force, its divine spark. It appeared to Moses as if the bush was on fire, but actually Moses was observing the divine spark of life that is present in all living things. This indeed was a miracle. Through this ordinary plant Moses had reached toward heaven, and God reached out to him.

The pace of life in our high-tech world is hectic. We are almost always in a hurry. It takes practice to slow down and observe the miracle of life. This section contains activities designed to sharpen our observation skills so that we, too, may be privileged to perceive the divine spark of life.

Opening the Eyes of the Blind

irchot hashahar (blessings of the dawn) are prayers traditionally recited by Jews upon awaking. One of these prayers
reads as follows: "Blessed are You, Adonai, our God, Ruler of the
universe, who gives sight to the blind (*pokei'ah ivrim*)." If only a
small minority of people are actually blind, why is this a prayer
to be recited by all Jews each day? In truth, there are many ways
in which a sighted person can be "blind." Perhaps we have
become blind to the natural world, taking it for granted and
ignoring its wonders. Perhaps we have become blind to the presence of God in the world and in our lives. We miss the miracles
present in every moment of our existence. *Pokei'ah ivrim*
reminds us to "open our eyes."

Ages: 7+

Hikers' Goals:

- to understand the *pokei'ah ivrim* blessing
- to appreciate the power of sight in viewing nature
  and its wonders

Procedure:
Everyone in the group chooses a partner. The *A* partners
close their eyes (to become "blind"). The *B* partners carefully
walk the *A* partners to a site of exceptional beauty or interest
and adjust their heads so their eyes will open on the selected
object or view. Just as a photographer can use a close-up or
panoramic lens, so, too, can the hikers guide their partners to

such sites as a small patch of colorful lichen or a wide open mountain vista.

The partners should then recite the *pokei'aḥ ivrim* prayer (or the leader can recite it on behalf of the group) to signify the "blind" partner's visual "awakening" to the natural world. The partners should decide in advance on a physical action that will restore the blind partner's sight—for example, saying, "When I tug on your earlobe, open your eyes." The *A* partners should open their eyes and take in the view. Have the partners switch roles and repeat as often as time and interest allow.

Emphasize that this activity should be done in silence and that partners must be trustworthy guides for each other.

Pokei'aḥ Ivrim Prayer

בָּרוּךְ אַתָּה, יְיָ אֱלֹהֵינוּ, מֶלֶךְ הָעוֹלָם, פּוֹקֵחַ עִוְרִים.

Baruch atah, Adonai Eloheinu, Melech haolam, pokei'aḥ ivrim.

Blessed are You, Adonai our God, Ruler of the universe, who gives sight to the blind.

Questions to Ask Hikers:

- How did it feel to be led around as if you were blind? To have your sight restored?

- What did you see? Had you noticed it earlier?

- How did it feel to see these images as a surprise gift? Was it different from when you saw them before?

- How did it feel to lead a blind person? What was it like to choose which sights to give your partner and to watch your partner's reactions? What was it like to be responsible for another person's safety?

Sh'ma: Listen

Sh'ma, the first word of Judaism's most important prayer, literally means "listen." If we want to perceive God's presence in the world, we must first create through our senses a receptive space within ourselves. While sight is our most developed sense, if we want to hear and understand the song of life, we must also develop the ability to listen attentively.

To help hikers listen, use the sounds of the Sh'ma itself. *Shhh* means "quiet yourself." *Mmmmm* means "listen and think about what you are hearing." *Ahhhh* means "understand what you have heard"—"SHHHMMMMAAAHHH"; in silence, listen, think about, and understand the sounds coming from God's creations in the world.

Ages: 7+

Hikers' Goals:

• to develop the ability to listen attentively

• be prepared to recite the Sh'ma in a prayer service

Procedure:

Activity 1: Find a quiet place on the trail. Instruct hikers to stand or sit quietly for one minute with their eyes closed and their hands raised in fists. Invite them to listen carefully and to put up one finger each time they hear a new sound—in other words, to count on their hands the number of different sounds they hear.

Ask hikers if they heard more sounds during this minute than during other times of the hike. Usually the answer will be yes. Invite them to continue to hike silently for a while and collect more sounds.

Activity 2: This activity demonstrates how we can increase our perceptiveness with intention. When standing near any source of natural sounds (e.g., a flowing stream, rustling leaves, crashing waves, a singing bird), have hikers first face the object and listen closely. Direct them to cup their ears with their hands, fingers extending upward, imitating deer or bunny ears. With their new, improved ears, hearing should increase close to 20 percent—even as much as 50 percent at night. They can play with removing and replacing their hands to vary the volume. Hint: If hikers place their hands in front of their ears, facing backward, this trick will help them hear sounds coming from behind them.

Following each activity, hikers should recite the Sh'ma.

Sh'ma Prayer

שְׁמַע יִשְׂרָאֵל, יְיָ אֱלֹהֵינוּ, יְיָ אֶחָד.

Sh'ma Yisrael Adonai Eloheinu Adonai ehad.

Listen, Israel, Adonai is our God, Adonai is One.

Questions to Ask Hikers:

• What sounds did you hear? Were they human, mechanical, or natural?

• How did the various sounds affect your body or your mood?

• Why do you think Jewish tradition says it is important to listen? What do other creatures and natural elements have to tell us? What can they teach us about God?

Bal Tash'hit and the Great Garbage Hunt

he prudent use of natural resources is a strong Jewish value. The mitzvah *bal tash'hit* (literally, "do not destroy") commands us not to waste natural resources or anything else and only to use that which we truly need. *Bal tash'hit* also commands us not to pollute the earth. Hikers can practice *bal tash'hit* not only by not littering, but also by picking up trash left by others. In this way, they are also practicing *tikkun olam*—helping to repair the world.

Ages: 4+

Hikers' Goals:

• to sharpen observation skills while walking slowly in the wilderness

• to practice the mitzvah *bal tash'hit*—to further the conservation and preservation of natural resources

Time: near the beginning of a hike

Materials:

• fifty-foot length of rope or string

• fifteen to forty objects not normally found in natural settings—some should be obvious, like aluminum cans, others more subtle, like toothpicks or pennies

• garbage bag

Procedure:

In advance of the activity and out of sight of the hikers, mark a course by laying the rope or string alongside trees and/or bushes. Place the objects on one side of the rope, on the ground and in bushes and trees. Some should be plainly visible and others partially hidden. All the items should be visible from the other side of the rope.

Bring the hikers to one end of the rope and explain that they must walk along the rope, on the side without the objects, and silently count how many objects they see. At the end of the rope, have them whisper to you how many items they saw. After everyone has had a turn, ask those who found five or more objects to raise their hands; then ten or more, fifteen, twenty, and so on. Most likely all the hikers will have their hands up at the start and will soon become surprised that they missed so many items. At this point, have them go through a second time. At the end of the second time, instruct them to pick up all the objects.

Variation: Put only ten to fifteen objects on the trail, and go through the procedure only once.

Debriefing:

Discuss the differences in the participants' approach to looking for objects each time they walked through. The second time, the hikers most likely walked more slowly and were more observant. Stress that this is how they should always hike along the trail.

Talk about how camouflage helps animals hide from prey by blending into the environment. Discuss the hasidic idea that God is hidden in works of creation. How can walking through nature with an enhanced awareness help us find God in works of creation?

Ask what we can do to fulfill the mitzvah of *bal tash'ḥit*. Take out the garbage bag and encourage the hikers to pick up litter as they continue the hike.

Observation: Moses Style

In order to properly attend to the needs of a flock, a shepherd must be acutely aware of the surrounding environment: the weather, possibilities for shelter, sources of food and water, and the presence of predators. If you have ever watched a campfire, for example, you know it takes quite a while until you notice the wood burning up. Moses, a shepherd, was so keenly observant that he spotted a bush that was burning without being consumed. Moses had to watch for a long time to make his observation. Perhaps that is one of the reasons God chose Moses: In him, God had a patient and observant leader.

Ages: 7+

Hikers' Goals:

• to observe the colors in nature with heightened awareness

Materials:

• paint samples from a paint or hardware store, cut into one-inch color squares

Procedure:

This activity is a great walking game. Tell the story of the burning bush, focusing on Moses' ability to observe. Give a paint chip to each hiker. Ask the hikers to match the color exactly to something they find along the way. Encourage them to be as observant as Moses.

Debriefing:

Examine together the items the hikers found to match their paint chips.

Questions to Ask Hikers:

- Did the Moses story influence the way you searched?
- Did your patience help you to observe more?
- Which colors were hardest to match? Why?

How Many Are Your Works!

There is a blessing in the morning prayer service that exclaims, *"Mah rabu ma'asecha Adonai! Kulam b'ḥochmah asita, malah ha'aretz kinyaneha"*—"How many are your works, God! All of them You created in wisdom; the world is filled with your possessions."

An ecosystem is a community of nature in which organisms combine with their environment to create an ecological unity. This activity invites hikers to discover the diversity and abundance of living creatures and natural elements within a given ecosystem.

Ages: 7+

Hikers' Goals:

- to recognize the capacity of a given ecological system to support life
- to sharpen observation skills
- to heighten appreciation of biodiversity

Materials:

- pennies, one for each hiker
- pieces of string cut into one-foot segments, one for each hiker

Procedure:

Discuss the text from the morning service noted above, emphasizing the prayer's appreciation of diversity, its assertion that everything was made in wisdom and therefore has value, and the notion that everything in the world ultimately belongs to God. With these ideas in mind, invite the hikers to participate in one or both of the following activities:

Activity 1: Give each of the hikers a penny; tell them to try to place as many nonliving things as possible on top of the coin. Allow five minutes for the hikers to look for the items.

Activity 2: Give each of the hikers a one-foot segment of string. Have them lay the string on the ground and ask them to count all the insects and other creatures that they can find along the string. Allow five minutes for this activity.

Debriefing:

Take a tour of each hiker's string. Ask each person to describe the items that were found (including the insects that may have crawled away). Or have hikers share with the group what each one put on the penny. Was anyone surprised by how many things were found? Ask hikers to evaluate and to try to explain the relative abundance or scarcity of living creatures at this site. What are the available resources, such as food, water, shelter? Think about temperature and the possible impact of predators or competitors. How may humans have an impact on this area? If we were searching in another season, would we find more or less?

What's in a Rainbow?

After the great flood subsided, God promised Noah and his descendants and all living creatures that God would never again bring a flood to destroy the earth. To seal the promise and mark this covenant, God placed a rainbow in the sky. When we see a rainbow, we remember God's covenant and recite the following blessing:

בָּרוּךְ אַתָּה, יְיָ אֱלֹהֵינוּ, מֶלֶךְ הָעוֹלָם, זוֹכֵר הַבְּרִית וְנֶאֱמָן בִּבְרִיתוֹ וְקַיָּם בְּמַאֲמָרוֹ.

Baruch atah, Adonai Eloheinu, Melech ha'olam, zocher habrit v'ne'eman bivrito v'kayam b'ma'amaro.

Blessed are You, Adonai our God, Ruler of the universe, who remembers the covenant, is faithful to it, and keeps God's promise.

The blessing reinforces the joy and delight we feel in seeing a rainbow, both because it is a sign of God's covenant and because it is a glorious example of the beauty of God's creation.

Ages: 7+

Hikers' Goals:

- to increase observation skills
- to understand that God promised never again to destroy the earth and that the rainbow is a sign of that promise
- to learn the blessing for seeing rainbows
- to learn the color order of rainbows
- to strengthen personal commitment to conservation

Procedure:

Tell the story of the rainbow as a sign of God's covenant never again to destroy the earth by flood. (Genesis 8:8-17) Teach the colors of the rainbow and their order: *R*ed, *O*range, *Y*ellow, *G*reen, *B*lue, *I*ndigo, and *V*iolet; use the mnemonic acronym ROY-G-BIV.

Have the hikers collect natural objects that make up the colors of a rainbow; remind them to take care not to kill or harm anything they collect. You may ask pairs of hikers to collect specific colors or just let the entire group search together. Leaves, slugs, rocks, berries, and so on, are some good examples of useful items for this project.

When the colored items have been collected, lay them out in the correct rainbow order, and lead the hikers in saying the rainbow blessing. Tell the participants that preserving the earth requires a partnership between God and humans; ask them to share promises they can make to protect the earth. Encourage them to think of rainbows as a reminder of the promises they make today.

Variation: Ask participants to gather as many different colors as they can in one minute. Have them group the colors together.

Questions to Ask Hikers:

- How is our rainbow different from or similar to the one in the sky?

- When you saw a rainbow before today, what did you think of? What will you think of when you see a rainbow from now on?

- Does knowing the rainbow blessing make you want to say it when you next see one?

- What other blessing might you recite when you see a rainbow?

Rav Kook Mystery Hunt

Abraham Isaac Kook (1865-1935) served as the first chief rabbi of the modern Ashkenazic Jewish community in Palestine. A deeply religious mystic who nevertheless took an active interest in human affairs, he was respected for his spiritual leadership, brilliant scholarship, and literary creativity.

One day Rav Kook was walking in the fields with a student, when the young man carelessly plucked a leaf off a branch. Visibly shaken by this act, Rav Kook turned to his companion and said gently, "Believe me when I tell you I never simply pluck a leaf or a blade of grass or any living thing unless I have to. Every part of the vegetable world is singing a song and breathing forth a secret of the divine mystery of creation." For the first time the young student understood the meaning of showing compassion to all living things.

In this activity hikers will search for hidden mysteries in nature and have the opportunity to show reverence for all life.

Ages: 7+

Hikers' Goals:

- to heighten respect for all living things
- to improve observation skills

Materials:

- Three-by-five-inch index cards with the following instruction printed on them:

Please find the following:

1. Something that matches your hair color

2. Evidence of a cycle in nature

3. Something that smells sweet

4. A sign of an animal

5. A seed

6. A sign of God (privately give thanks)

7. Something that reminds you of your family

Important note: Do not kill or pluck any living thing during this activity. In some cases you might need to leave something where you found it; if that happens, bring the group to the object.

Procedure:

Read the story about Rav Kook and discuss its meaning. Distribute a "Rav Kook Mystery Hunt" card to each hiker or have hikers pair up. Explain that they will have a chance to look for some of the mysteries in nature. They should collect as many items on the cards as they can find, but remind them not to pluck or kill anything as they gather the items.

Questions to Ask Hikers:

• Do you believe that the mysteries of nature are a sign of God's existence?

• What did Rav Kook mean when he said, "Every part of the vegetable world is singing a song and breathing forth a secret of the divine mystery of creation"?

• Have you ever heard the song Rav Kook was talking about? Have you heard it in your heart?

Sitting like Elijah

he Bible states that Elijah stood on Mount Horeb in Israel waiting to hear God. He waited through a great wind that tore rocks from the mountain; he waited through an earthquake; he waited through a fire. God did not appear in any of these natural phenomena. After waiting on the mountain for a long while, Elijah finally heard God's voice in a whisper. (I Kings 19:9-14)

Unlike Elijah, most of us have difficulty staying in one place, waiting to be touched by God. Always on the move, we often miss opportunities to experience the wonders around us, even on a hike. In this activity, hikers learn to sit patiently and allow the wonders of creation to come to them.

Ages: 10+

Hikers' Goals:

• to gain a deeper experience of one place

• to connect personal experiences in nature with the experience of Elijah

Materials:

• Bible

• paper or notepad and writing implements

Procedure:

Read or tell the story of Elijah on Mount Horeb. Ask hikers to relate the longest time they have sat quietly in one spot in nature (or anywhere) and what they experienced. Explain that by staying in one place, we can see and experience things that we would miss if we were moving. You may want to draw a comparison between how much more one sees when walking than when driving. Distribute paper and writing implements, and instruct hikers to find a nearby spot where they can sit comfortably.

Sitting like Elijah requires hikers to stay in one spot while being attentive and quiet. While sitting like Elijah, the hikers should record everything their senses pick up during a period of ten to fifteen minutes. They may also include their feelings that they become aware of.

Questions to Ask Hikers:

- Have you ever felt the presence of God or the power of nature as Elijah did? What were the circumstances?

- What elements of nature did you sense while sitting like Elijah that you did not sense during other parts of the hike?

- How long do you think you would be able to sit quietly by yourself?

- Did you feel the presence of God or the power of nature in this activity?

CHAPTER 3

One Glorious Chain of Love

God instructs us to revere life. In order to follow God's instructions, we first must learn how the world around us works. We can gain an appreciation of the interconnectedness of all life by studying the cycles of nature—such as water and air cycles—and the process of the transference of energy through food chains.

The activities in this chapter focus on ecological relationships and cycles in nature. A growing understanding of ecology can lead to actions of loving-kindness toward the earth and the living plants and animals we share it with.

"One glorious chain of love, of giving and receiving, unites all living things. All things exist in continuous reciprocal activity—one for all, all for one. None has power, or means, for itself; each gives in order to receive, and receives in order to give, and finds therein the fulfillment of the purpose of its existence."

—"THIRD LETTER," *The Nineteen Letters About Judaism*
RABBI SAMSON RAPHAEL HIRSCH (1808-88)

Yotzer Or: Sunshine Powers Life

Judaism recognizes the centrality to life of the sun and its light. Yotzer Or, the morning prayer that celebrates the daily renewal of creation, praises God as creator of light. Our ancestors understood 2,000 years ago what we now know scientifically—life cannot exist if the sun ceases its daily cycle. Yotzer Or articulates our thankfulness with these words:

בָּרוּךְ אַתָּה, יְיָ אֱלֹהֵינוּ, מֶלֶךְ הָעוֹלָם, יוֹצֵר אוֹר וּבוֹרֵא חֹשֶׁךְ,
עוֹשֶׂה שָׁלוֹם וּבוֹרֵא אֶת־הַכֹּל. הַמֵּאִיר לָאָרֶץ וְלַדָּרִים עָלֶיהָ
בְּרַחֲמִים.

*Baruch atah, Adonai Eloheinu, Melech ha'olam, yotzer or uvorei
ḥoshech, oseh shalom uvorei et-hakol. Hamei'ir la'aretz v'ladarim alei'hah
b'raḥamim.*

Blessed is the one who forms light and creates darkness, who makes peace and creates all things, who with mercy sheds light upon the earth and upon all who dwell on it.

Green plants that convert sunlight into food through the process of photosynthesis are called producers. Animals who eat only plants are primary consumers and are called herbivores. Animals who eat other animals are secondary consumers and are called carnivores. Plants and animals that feed on dead plants and animals and convert them back into the soil are called decomposers (e.g., bacteria, worms, fungi, slugs). All living things receive their energy from the light of the sun, either directly, like the producers, or indirectly, like consumers and decomposers.

This activity teaches about the sun and the cycle of life that depends upon it.

Ages: 10+

Hikers' Goals:

- to understand the importance of the sun as our energy source
- to learn the role and significance of producers, consumers, and decomposers

Materials:

- index cards with one of the following pictures on each one: sun, rabbit, bear, mushroom, tree
- three cards with arrows

Procedure:

On the ground, create a circle four feet or larger in diameter, using rocks for the circumference. Using sticks, divide the circle into three equal triangular wedges.

Without an explanation, divide the hikers into three groups and send them to look for one of the following (preferably items they do not have to pick in order to collect):

- green vegetation
- a sign of an animal
- a decomposer (e.g., worms, slugs, mushrooms, fungi)

When the hikers bring back what they have collected, place the green things (producers) in one triangle, the signs of animals (consumers) in another, and the decomposers in the third. Add the picture cards: the sun in the middle of the circle, the rabbit and bear in the consumer triangle, the tree in the producer triangle, and the mushroom in the decomposer triangle. Teach the miracle of the life cycle as explained above.

Questions to Ask Hikers:

- How do we humans get the sun's energy into our bodies?

- What would happen to the earth if decomposers were absent?

- Why do you think God's first creation was to separate light from darkness?

- Can you think of any living thing that is not dependent on the sun for its survival?

Teva (Nature) Tips

Numerous texts in the Bible and other Jewish writings reveal that our ancestors had intimate knowledge of the plants and animals around them and of humans' impact on the natural environment. Ancient Jewish agrarian laws generally ensure proper and efficient use of the land and protection of the land and its resources.

In Exodus 23:10-11, for example, we read, "For six years you can sow and harvest your land, but in the seventh year you must let it rest and lie fallow," a practice that replenishes the soil and increases its fertility.

Leviticus 19:23-25 tells us, "When you come to the land and plant trees for food, do not eat the fruit for three years; it is forbidden. Fruit from the fourth year shall be set aside for God. In the fifth year, you may eat." This agricultural tenet ensures development of a healthy plant; the tree's energies may go to building a strong root and branch system before they are needed to replenish harvested fruit.

In addition, the Talmud includes a prohibition against the breeding of small cattle in the Land of Israel (*Baba Kama* 79b). Such animals were known to eat grass to the roots; devoid of roots to grip it, the soil would suffer water and wind erosion.

This activity is designed for hikers to relearn some of the knowledge of nature that our ancestors had. The word *rabbi* literally means "teacher." Hikers will all become "*teva* (nature) rabbis" and will teach each other *teva* tips as they walk along the trail.

Ages: 9+

Hikers' Goals:

- to learn the diversity of a particular bioregion
- to become knowledgeable in at least one piece of natural history
- to teach and learn from each other

Location: a trail whose natural history is known to you

Procedure:

Conduct a brief ceremony to turn the hikers into *teva* rabbis. (For example: "Repeat after me: 'I am now a *teva* rabbi. I promise to uphold the laws of ecology, say the rainbow blessing whenever I see a rainbow, and never to step on bugs or spiders.'")

Divide the group into pairs. Take one pair of hikers up the trail until you find something for them to teach—a pine tree, for example. Teach the pair some basic information about pine trees; each of those hikers is now Rabbi Pine Tree. Call for a second pair to leave the main group and hike up the trail, stopping at Rabbi Pine Tree's station. Rabbi Pine Tree teaches the new pair of hikers about pine trees, and then this pair continues with you along the trail until you come to another topic to teach—a bird's nest, for example. This pair becomes Rabbi Bird's Nest. A third pair of hikers stops first at Rabbi Pine Tree, continues on to Rabbi Bird's Nest, and then continues with you to a third station.

Once all the pairs have passed Rabbi Pine Tree, Rabbi Pine Tree continues to Rabbi Bird's Nest. This process continues until every pair of rabbis has taught and learned from every other pair of rabbis.

STATION SUGGESTIONS:

Rabbi Tree Trees are an important part of most ecosystems. Their roots help hold soil in place, preventing erosion from rain and wind. Their leaves photosynthesize light from the sun to make food for the tree and for primary consumers. Their leaves also help clean the air by breathing in carbon dioxide and breathing out oxygen. When trees are cut down, the ecosystem can drastically change and may not recover for many years. (You can add specific facts about trees indigenous to your area.)

Rabbi Fern Ferns grow mostly in moist areas, but some have adapted to growing in direct sunlight. Ferns are ancient plants that were contemporaries of the dinosaurs. Instead of seeds, they multiply through spores, which grow on the underside of their leaves.

Questions rabbis can ask:

- What qualities of ferns have allowed them to survive for so many eons?

- Can any of these qualities help human beings in our evolutionary survival?

Rabbi Bird's Nest Finding a bird's nest (or even seeing a bird) on the trail presents a wonderful opportunity to have your rabbis teach Torah. Read the following selection from Deuteronomy (22:6-7): "If, along the road, you chance upon a bird's nest, in any tree or on the ground, with fledglings or eggs and the mother sitting over the fledglings or on the eggs, do not take the mother together with her young. Let the mother go, and take only the young, in order that you may fare well and have a long life."

Nahmanides (the 13th-century Spanish mystic Rabbi Moses ben Nahman) said, in his *Commentary on the Torah*, that scripture does not permit a destructive act that will cause the extinction of a species, even when it has permitted the ritual slaughtering of that species. Someone who kills the mother and the offspring in one day or who takes them while they are free to fly away is considered as one who has destroyed the species.

Questions rabbis can ask:

- Do you have to take an egg or a chick from a nest you see?
- Why is it okay to take the young and not the mother bird?
- Why would you "fare well" if you follow this mitzvah?
- Why would it be bad for you if you broke this mitzvah?

Rabbi Flower All flowers manufacture seeds. Explore the flower and find where you think the seeds grow. The two most important parts of a flower are the pistil and stamen. Pollen from the pistil is transferred to the stamen through a process called pollination, which results in the making of a seed. Often the pollen from one blossom is carried to and pollinates a different one, creating a genetically different type of flower. The beauty and scent of flowers lure pollinators—such as bees, moths, insects, or birds—to them. When the pollinator sips the flower's nectar, pollen sticks to its body and comes off when it visits another flower.

Questions rabbis can ask:

- What might pollinate this flower: a bee, insect, moth, or bird?
- How would pollination occur with this flower?
- Where do you expect to see the next flower growing? (Look for where the seeds might fall or be blown to after they have formed.)

Rabbi Insect Insects have six legs and are food for many bigger insects, birds, spiders, amphibians, and small mammals. Insects pollinate flowers, and some, such as ants, are important decomposers. They should never be stepped on or thoughtlessly killed. Share the following teaching: "Rabbi Yehudah said...everything God created in this world has a purpose—even the things that humans may consider to be unnecessary, such as flies, fleas, and mosquitoes, are part of the creation." (*Genesis Rabbah* 10:7 or 8)

Questions rabbis can ask:

- Can you think of two good things mosquitoes do?
- How can you get an insect out of your house without killing it?
- Name one animal, insect or plant that you don't like. Can you think of a purpose it has in the "circle of life"?

Rabbi Fungus Fungi are decomposers that grow on rocks and trees. They play a critical role in the life cycle of the ecosystem by helping break down dead plants and rocks into soil. Fungi come in many shapes and colors. Sometimes they combine with algae in a symbiotic relationship to make lichen (pronounced "liken"). Comic relief: They say that Freddy Fungus took a "lichen" to Alice Algae, but the last anyone heard, their relationship was on the rocks (ha, ha!).

> *A game that Rabbi Fungus can teach:* One person is fungus, and the partner is algae. They sit back to back with arms interlocked at the elbows. The object of the game is for them to stand up together while still attached at the elbows. The fungus chants, "fungus, fungus, fungus" and the algae chants, "algae, algae, algae" as they try to stand. When they succeed, they yell out, "lichen!"

Rabbi Trail Jewish law is called *Halachah*, which means "the way"; *halachot* refers to individual laws. Just as *Halachah* provides a designated path through life for those who follow it, trails provide a way through the wilderness. If you step off the hiking trail and wander wherever you want, you can cause unnecessary erosion that may cause damage to the environment.

Questions rabbis can ask:

- What are some of the *halachot* for the area we are hiking in?

- Can you think of some environmental *halachot* for you to follow in your life?

- What happens when we do not follow Jewish teachings on the environment?

Questions to Ask Hikers:

- What did you like about being a *teva* rabbi?

- Did your fellow rabbis teach you things you didn't know before?

- Were you surprised to learn that the Torah contains teachings about how to behave in natural settings?

- How is learning from others on the trail different from learning from a book or in a classroom?

Miriam's Water-Cycle Imagery

As a desert people, the ancient Israelites understood the value of water. At times the lack of water forced them temporarily to leave the land of Israel. The prophet Miriam is closely connected with water. According to legend, Miriam's Well was the Israelites' source of water while they traveled through the wilderness. This magical well followed them, providing water and sustaining their lives.

Similarly, the water cycle, which comprises evaporation, condensation, and precipitation, sustains our lives. This is known as a closed cycle. Water is never lost or gained, it just travels through different parts of the water cycle. The water used by the Israelites in the desert is, for the most part, the same water in use today.

Ages: 12+

Hikers' Goals:

- to understand the water cycle
- to learn the connection between Miriam and water

Location: a body of water to sit by

Procedure: Read the guided imagery below to the hikers.

Instructions to reader:

1. Recite the imagery slowly, in an even voice.

2. .... means pause; _____ means long pause

Note: This meditation assumes the participants are near a stream. Vary the images to suit the particular environment.

Lie down and get comfortable.... Close your eyes.... Listen to the gurgling of the water.... Listen to its different sounds.... Become aware of your breath.... Count five normal breaths._____ Take a full breath and slowly let it out._____ Tension flows away from you like the flowing water._____

Imagine you are a drop of water flowing in the stream._____ You are surrounded by millions of other water drops, part of Egypt's great Nile River.... You are moving toward the sea.... How does it feel to be part of this current?_____ As you flow along, you see a large city and are pushed into a still eddy surrounded by reeds.... You feel a basket being placed upon you and the surrounding water drops.... You help support the basket.... Inside the basket is a baby.... Is it easy or hard to support this basket?_____ Soon the basket is lifted up by a pair of hands as you cling to its side.... You see the face of a young girl watching from behind the reeds.... You look into her eyes.... You know this face._____ You feel the hot sun on you.... The sun pulls on you and it is hard to hold on to the basket. You lose your grip and are whisked away into the sky._____

In the air you are transformed into water vapor and you float aimlessly.... You enjoy this feeling of freedom.____ It begins to cool down, and with other water vapor you form a cloud.... As part of the cloud, you make your way toward the Sea of Reeds.... The air becomes colder, and you become heavier.... You are changing back into a drop of water, and the cloud can no longer hold you.... You become a raindrop and splash into the Sea of Reeds.... You move slowly in and out with the tide.____ You pass the time observing beautiful fish and coral.____

The wind begins to blow.... You and all the drops around you are picked up by what feels like a giant hand.... You are taken farther out to sea.... You look back and see a wide path of mud and thousands of people hurrying across.____ Hundreds of chariots follow after them, but their wheels get stuck in the mud.... The wind stops, and you and all your neighbor drops flow back and cover the chariots and charioteers.____ You rise near the surface of the sea and see the same young girl you saw before.... Now she is an adult, and with her tambourine she is leading the people in song and dance.... You want to watch this woman, but you rise too close to the surface and evaporate into the air.____

You are now floating over the desert.... How does the world look from up high?____ After a while, you come upon the same group of people you saw earlier.____ The girl is now an old woman and is about to die.... She is sitting next to a well. It is *her* well, Miriam's well.... She is surrounded by many people.... As her soul leaves her body, all the water in the wells and streams of the desert flee the earth and accompany her soul.... The people below are crying and arguing, as you and the surrounding water vapor are whisked away by a strong wind that takes you to the north.... As you fly farther north, you condense back into a drop and join other drops to form a cloud.... It becomes colder and colder until finally you turn into a snowflake and gently fall to the earth. You become part of a glacier, where you remain for a long, long time.____ How does it feel to be lying in quiet solitude for so long?____

The air is warming up and the snow and ice around you are melting.... You also melt and flow into a river.... You flow south through many different rivers.____ Finally you become part of a stream on whose bank people are lying down, listening to a story.... As you float by, you are scooped up in a cup; you see yourself while a person drinks you.____ You are now back to yourself.____

Listen to the different sounds of the creek.____

Remember the places you have been to and the images you have seen.____ When you are ready, open your eyes and sit up.

Variations:

• Write another story about Miriam and water.

• Draw a picture of Miriam's well or make a nature picture using watercolors.

Questions to Ask Hikers:

• What part of the story made the clearest picture in your mind?

• Did you feel part of the water cycle? Which part?

• What did you learn about the water cycle?

• After Miriam's death, the magic well stopped giving water. Perhaps without her, the Israelites forgot the practice of conservation and protection of water. What can individuals and communities do to ensure that our water remain clean and plentiful?

CHAPTER 4

Trees:
The Torah of Life

udaism has long recognized the importance of trees. In Deuteronomy 20:19-20, God expressly prohibits cutting down fruit trees, even in times of war. A well-known *midrash* in Leviticus Rabbah (25:3) teaches that one way to walk in the footsteps of God is to plant trees. The tree is also an important metaphor in many Jewish texts. For example, the prophet Jeremiah wrote:

Blessed is one who trusts in God,
Whose trust is in God alone.
That person shall be like a tree planted by waters,
sending forth its roots by a stream:
It does not sense the coming of heat,
Its leaves are forever fresh;
It has no care in a year of drought,
It does not cease to yield fruit.

—JEREMIAH 17:7-8

Our best known tree metaphor compares the Torah to an *etz hayyim*—a "tree of life"—implying that Jews could not exist without the Torah. As we learn more about the natural world, a new metaphor is born: Trees are the Torah of life. Just as Jews cannot survive without Torah, no one can survive without trees, the lungs of the world and the backbone of many ecosystems. They also provide people with shade, food, medicine, and building materials.

The spiritual significance of trees was acknowledged by the great hasidic master Rabbi Nahman of Bratslav, who believed that the divine spark of life found in trees and plants can help elevate prayers to reach God.

When Will and Grace Are Joined

n his classic work *I and Thou*, Martin Buber wrote that there are two types of relationships: "I-it" and "I-thou." In an "I-it" relationship, one relates to another person, to nature, or to God as an object or in reference to the function each performs for the person. For example, if the sight of a tree prompts thoughts of how you would like a wooden hot tub in your backyard or brings to mind only the name of the tree, then you are having an "I-it" relationship with the tree.

Buber explains that most of the time we relate to nature and people—even family members and friends—in an "I-it" fashion. An "I-thou" relationship happens only in rare moments when, as he puts it, "will and grace are joined." It is the moment when one accepts and honors the true essence and the wholeness of a person, nature, or God.

In this activity hikers have the opportunity to have an "I-thou" moment with a tree—a moment during which they see the "life force of the plant" and its "divine spark."

Traditionally, Jews are allowed to carry objects on Shabbat only within certain boundaries. An *eruv* (the literal meaning is "mixing") is a boundary placed around the perimeter of a community that turns the community into a single public space, allowing traditional Jews to carry on Shabbat within that space. Here the hikers will create a "spiritual *eruv*."

Ages: 14+

Hikers' Goals:

- to learn about Martin Buber's concept of "I–thou" and "I-it"
- to experience an "I-thou" moment with a tree

Materials:

- a ten-foot piece of string

Procedure:

Begin with a quiet activity, such as a brief silent walk, or following an activity such as "Sitting like Elijah." Explain Buber's notion of "I-it" and "I-thou." Divide the group into ḥevruta (learning partners) pairs. Ask the partners to share with each other an "I-it" relationship they have had recently and an "I-thou" relationship they have experienced.

Have the pairs read the following passage from Martin Buber's *I and Thou.*

I can contemplate a tree. I can accept it as a picture: a ridged pillar in a flood of light, or splashes of green traversed by the gentleness of the blue silver ground. I can feel it as a movement: the flowing veins around the sturdy core, the sucking of the roots, the breathing of the leaves, the infinite commerce with earth and air—and the growing itself in its darkness. I can assign it to a species and observe it as an instance, with an eye to its construction and its way of life. I can overcome its uniqueness and form so rigorously that I can recognize it only as an expression of law—those laws according to which a constant opposition of forces is continually adjusted, or those laws according to which the elements mix and separate. I can dissolve it into a number, into a pure relation between numbers, and externalize it. Throughout all of this the tree, the tree remains my object and has its place and its time span, its kind and condition. But it can also happen, if will and grace are joined, that as I contemplate the tree, I am drawn into a relation, and the tree ceases to be an It. The power of exclusiveness has seized me.

After reading the passage, each *ḥevruta* pair should discuss its meaning. Then, individually, hikers are invited to encircle themselves and a tree with the string for fifteen minutes to create a spiritual *eruv*. During this time the hikers should try to enter into an "I-thou" moment with the tree by listening to the sounds of the tree, feeling the tree, and contemplating other ways that one can create this relationship.

Variation: Bring a drawing pad to the tree and, during the fifteen minutes, hikers can draw a picture of the tree or write a poem, story, or song to the tree.

Questions to Ask Hikers:

• What did you discuss in your *ḥevruta* regarding the Martin Buber text?

• What was your experience with the tree?

• Did making the *eruv* enrich your experience, make it more sacred?

Meeting Trees

Tree imagery abounds in Judaism. One *midrash* tells us that if we want to follow in the steps of God, we must plant trees (*Leviticus Rabbah* 25:3). Another *midrash* teaches that if we are in the act of planting trees and the messiah comes, we should first finish planting our tree and then greet the messiah (*Avot de-Rabbi Natan* 31b).

This activity builds on the metaphor introduced at the beginning of this chapter: Trees are the Torah of life.

Ages: 6+

Hikers' Goals:

• to become familiar with Jewish stories about trees

• to build a relationship with trees

Materials:

• blindfolds

• drawing materials

Procedure:

Take hikers to a spot where there are plenty of trees. Ask them if they know any Jewish stories about trees or why the Torah is called the tree of life. Ask them if they think the metaphor "Trees are the Torah of life" makes sense. Share one of the following stories about trees.

How to Be Godly

Rabbi Judah son of Simon began by quoting the Bible: "After Adonai your God shall you walk. And onto God shall you cleave." (Deuteronomy 13:5) Rabbi Judah said, But how can a person walk after God, the One of whom it is written: "Your way was in the sea and your path in the great waters"? (Psalm 77:20) And how can flesh-and-blood go up into heaven to cleave to God, the One of whom it is written: "God's throne was fiery flames"? (Daniel 7:9)

But God, from the very beginning of the creation of the world, was before all else occupied with planting, as is proved by the text, "And Adonai your God first planted a garden in Eden." (Genesis 2:8) Therefore, when you enter the land, occupy yourself with nothing else but planting. Thus it is written, "When you come into the land, then you shall plant."

(Leviticus Rabbah 25:3)

Honi and the Carob Tree

One day Honi the sage was walking through the fields near his home in the Galilee. He happened upon an old man planting a carob tree. Honi asked the man, "Why are you planting that carob tree? You will never get any fruit from it." Honi knew that it takes seventy years or more for a carob tree to bear fruit; the old man would be long dead before he could reap any harvest from the tree.

The old man continued planting as he said to Honi, "Just as my grandfather planted trees so that I would enjoy their fruit, so I am planting this tree for my grandchildren."

When the old man left, Honi chuckled and said to himself, "Maybe my grandchildren will benefit from my resting in the shade of this gigantic tree." Honi then sat down next to the carob seedling, closed his eyes, and fell asleep.

Some time later, Honi awoke; he had felt a chill and guessed that a cloud had moved across the sun. He opened his eyes and—lo and behold!—the seedling had turned into a big, beautiful carob tree whose shade had blocked the sun's warmth. "What a crazy dream I'm in," he said to himself. He pinched himself to wake up, but all the pinch did was leave a painful welt on his skin.

Just then, Honi noticed an old man collecting carob pods from the tree. Honi asked the man if he was the one who had planted the tree.

"It was my grandfather who planted this tree seventy years ago," answered the old man.

What had happened hit Honi like a ton of bricks. He jumped up and started to run away. "Hey!" cried the old man. "Where are you going?"

"I must go," cried Honi. "I've got lots of trees to plant!"

—ADAPTED FROM BABYLONIAN TALMUD *Ta'anit* 23A

Divide the hikers into pairs. One person is blindfolded and led by the other person to a tree. (This should be demonstrated before sending the hikers out on their own.) When the blindfolded people "meet" the trees, they should touch, smell, and become familiar with "their" tree so they will be able to distinguish it from other trees in the vicinity. Encourage hikers to spend at least two minutes at their tree.

When they are ready, the guides lead the blindfolded people back to the starting place. The blindfolds are removed, and the people try to find their tree. Partners then switch roles. After all the hikers have found their trees, invite them to spend five minutes with their tree. During this time they can make a wish for their tree, or they can breathe with their tree, giving it the gift of carbon dioxide, which trees need, and breathing in the oxygen that trees give to us.

Variation: Have participants imagine themselves as trees. They should ask themselves, "Do I have roots, leaves, branches, a trunk?" Have them draw a picture of themselves as a tree.

Questions to Ask Hikers:

- What are your feelings toward your tree?

- What does your tree teach you about your life?

- If trees are truly the Torah of life, then what can we do to ensure the future of healthy forests?

Build a Tree of Life

t is a tree of life for those who hold fast to it, and all of its supporters are happy. Its ways are pleasant ways and all its paths, peaceful." (Proverbs 3:17–18)

Throughout the generations, Jews have studied, interpreted, and struggled over the meaning of the words of the Torah. The study of Torah is an attempt to step into the text and gain a greater understanding of ourselves, our world, and God.

In much the same way, scientific inquiry does this in connection to the natural world. By building a "tree of life," participants will learn about the life of a tree. This activity is adapted from "Build a Tree" in Joseph Cornell's *Sharing the Joy of Nature*.

Ages: 8+

Hikers' Goals:

- to learn tree biology through role playing

- to make a connection between the Torah and trees

Procedure:

To build a tree, hikers act out the various parts: the roots, heartwood, sapwood, cambium layer, and bark. The heartwood provides strength and support for the tree. The roots anchor the tree in the ground and draw water up from the ground. The sapwood carries water from the roots to the leaves. The cambium layer transports food from the leaves to the rest of the tree, and the bark protects the tree.

NOW BUILD YOUR TREE:

Heartwood—Choose two or three tall or strong hikers and have them stand with their backs to each other. Tell them, "You are the heartwood—the inner core, the strength of the tree. You have been around a long time—you are, in fact, dead; your thousands of little tubes that used to carry water upward and food downward are now all clogged with resin and pitch. But you are well preserved!" Tell the heartwood players to stand tall and strong; when they get the signal from you, they should thump a heartbeat rhythm on their chests as a symbol of their strength.

Roots—Ask a few hikers to sit with their backs against the heartwood and their legs stretched out. Tell them, "You are the roots. There are hundreds of roots in a tree. You grow outward or down, like branches, but underground. You help the tree grip the ground and give it balance; your job is to absorb water in the soil for the tree's nourishment." Tell the root players to bring their knees to their chests and that at your signal they should repeat this chant: "Water, water, water; slurp, slurp, slurp."

Sapwood—Choose enough people to form a complete circle around the heartwood and roots. Have them crouch down and warn them not to step on the roots. Tell them, "You are the sapwood or xylem. You bring life to the tree by drawing water up from the roots and lifting it to the tree's highest branches. You are able to lift hundreds of gallons of water a day; in some trees you do this at speeds of over 100 miles an hour." Tell them that at the appropriate time, they should come out of their crouch, stand up, throw their hands in the air, and say, "Water, water, water, wheee!'"

Cambium/phloem—These players should form a circle around the sapwood, facing the heartwood. Ask them to stretch their arms over their heads and turn their hands into leaves. Tell them, "You are the part of the tree that helps it to grow, causing the rings that we see in tree trunks. When the leaves photosynthesize sunlight into food, the phloem carries the food around inside the tree." Tell them that at your signal they should shout, "We're hungry, we're hungry," while shaking their fingers/ leaves. Then they should bring their fingers to their bellies while chanting, "Food, food, food."

Bark—Ask the remaining hikers to circle the entire tree, facing out, away from the heartwood. Tell them, "You are the tree's protective layer, its skin. You protect the tree from insects, fire, extreme temperatures, and humans with carving knives." Tell them to get in an offensive lineman's blocking stance and, at your signal, to grunt or growl as a warning to anyone or anything that would harm the tree.

Like a choir leader, signal each part of the tree to begin its performance, one by one, until the whole tree is alive with music and rhythm:

Heartwood: Beat rhythm on their chest.

Roots: "Water, water, water; slurp, slurp, slurp."

Sapwood/xylem: "Water, water, water, wheee!"

Cambium/phloem: "We're hungry, we're hungry; food, food, food."

Bark: Grunt or growl.

When the entire tree has come to life, turn yourself into a bark beetle and stage an "attack." The bark, as the tree's protector, should be able to mount a successful defense against the predator.

Tell the hikers that the next time they see, kiss, or touch the Torah, they should remember the trees they visited and the tree they built on their nature journey.

Questions to Ask Hikers:

• How was the tree we built like the Torah?

• Why is the Torah called the tree of life?

• Does it make sense to you to call trees the Torah of life?

CHAPTER 5

Making Makom: Places in Nature

acob's first encounter with the divine occurred while he was traveling through the wilderness on his way to Haran. He stopped to sleep and, his head upon a stone, he dreamed of a ladder that reached into heaven, and he heard the voice of God.

Jacob was not the only one to experience the presence of God while in the wilderness. It was in the wilderness that Moses encountered God at the burning bush, that Elijah heard the small, still voice upon Mount Horeb, that Hagar met with an angel of God, and that the Jewish people received the Torah.

Despite the pivotal events that took place there, Jacob's precise location at the time of his dream is not mentioned in the Bible. Instead, the Torah just calls it *makom*, or "place." Biblical language is usually spare; when a word is repeated, it is often because a point is being made. In this short passage, the word *makom* is repeated three times. One explanation for this repetition is that it is intended to emphasize that this sacred *makom*, this place where humans can experience God, is not confined to the one specific place where Jacob camped but rather, it can be anywhere where one is open to the divine presence.

"Making *makom*," the creation of a spiritual place, is often the climax of a hike or wilderness experience. This section includes activities designed to give hikers tools to help them create their own *makom*.

Alone in the Wilderness

For many hikers, the thought of spending time alone in the wilderness can be both awe-inspiring and terrifying. This exercise invites hikers to open themselves to these feelings by making their own *makom*. Thorough preparation before such an experience and effective debriefing afterward are essential.

Ages: 13+

Hikers' Goals:

- to feel comfortable being alone in nature
- to learn techniques that can help make a spiritual connection to God

Materials:

- string, journals, and writing instruments

Procedure:

Have hikers sit in a circle and ask them to share an experience of being alone in nature. Read, tell, or have hikers study the biblical account of Jacob's dream and one or more of the biblical texts below.

Invite hikers to make their own *makom* by taking part in a "lone sit." Seat hikers along a trail, river, or ridge—one by one—in spots where they cannot see one another. (Never leave younger children alone by the water's edge.) Give hikers a ten-foot length of string to construct a "spiritual *eruv*" (see "When Will and Grace Are Joined" on page 39). They should stay within this circle during their sit. Give them a journal or other writing material to record their thoughts and feelings. Assure them that you or another leader will be within shouting distance at all times.

Pick up the hikers individually when the allotted time is up.

The amount of time depends on the age of the participants. On a day hike, thirty to forty-five minutes is good for older hikers; for younger ones, fifteen minutes may be enough. On an extended wilderness trip, one or two hours is good for a first-time lone sit. Experienced hikers can build up to a period of twenty-four hours or more. Remember, Moses was alone on the mountain for forty days—twice!

Note: It is helpful to acknowledge to young hikers that lone sits may seem boring at first. They may benefit from concrete suggestions as to what to do during the lone sit, such as writing down thoughts or drawing pictures related to the natural environment surrounding them.

Biblical Texts

Jacob's Dream

And Jacob went out from Be'er Sheva and traveled toward Haran. He reached a certain place (*makom*) and camped there because the sun had set. He took one of the stones from that place (*makom*) and he put it under his head and lay down in that place (*makom*) and slept. He dreamed and—behold—a ladder was set upon the earth, and the top of it reached to heaven. Angels of God were going up and coming down on it. And Adonai stood beside him and said, "I am Adonai, God of Abraham, your father, and God of Isaac." (Genesis 28:10–13)

The Burning Bush

Moses was the shepherd for the flock of Jethro, his father-in-law, who was the priest of Midian. Moses led the flock into the wilderness and came to Horeb, the mountain of God. An angel of God appeared to him in a flame of fire in the midst of a bush. He looked, and—behold—the bush burned with fire, but the bush was not consumed. Moses said, "I will turn aside and see this great sight, why the bush is not burned." When God saw that he turned aside to look, God called to him out of the bush, and said, "Moses, Moses." He answered, "Here I am." And God said, "Don't come near. Take your shoes off from your feet, because the place which you stand on is holy ground." God said, "I am the God of your father, the God of Abraham, the God of Isaac, the God of Jacob." And Moses hid his face for he was afraid to gaze at God. (Exodus 3:1–6)

Hagar and Ishmael Cast Out into the Wilderness

Abraham rose up early in the morning, and took some bread and a bottle of water and gave them to Hagar. He placed them on her shoulder, together with the child, and sent her away. She left and wandered in the wilderness of Be'er Sheva. And the bottle was empty, and she cast the child under one of the shrubs. She went and sat down far away from him, the distance of a bow shot. For she said, "Let me not see the death of the child." And she sat opposite him and lifted up her voice and cried. God heard the voice of the lad, and the angel of God called to Hagar out of heaven and said to her, "What ails you, Hagar? Fear not; God has heard the voice of the lad where he is. Arise, lift up the lad and hold him in your hand; for I will make him a great nation." And God opened her eyes, and she saw a well of water; and she filled the bottle with water and gave the lad a drink. And God was with the lad; and he grew and lived in the wilderness and became an archer. (Genesis 21:14–20)

Moses Climbing Mount Sinai and Receiving the Torah

Adonai said to Moses, "Come up to Me on the mountain, and be there. I will give you the tablets of stone and the Torah and the commandments which I have written, that you may teach them." Moses rose up with Joshua; and Moses went up onto the mountain of God.... Moses went up the mountain, and the cloud covered the mountain. The glory of Adonai rested on Mount Sinai, and the cloud covered it for six days. On the seventh day, He called to Moses out of the midst of the cloud. And the sight of the glory of Adonai was like a devouring fire on the top of the mountain in the eyes of the children of Israel. Moses went into midst of the cloud and went up the mountain; and Moses was on the mountain for forty days and forty nights. (Exodus 24:12–19)

Debriefing:

- Gather in a circle and have hikers share what they experienced during the lone sit. Set a proper tone. (See "Moses' Staff" on page 6.)

- Discuss with the hikers how they can make *makom* in their homes.

As You Walk on Your Way

ollowing the Sh'ma is the Ve'ahavta paragraph. It states that one should always be mindful of loving God and doing God's commandments, including *uv'lecht'cha vaderech—* while you are walking on your way. This activity teaches some commandments and a bit of natural history while hikers "walk on their way."

Hikers' Goals:

- to be quiet and alone in nature

- to pay attention to sights they might otherwise miss

Location: A trail or path, without many side paths, where you can walk for ten to thirty minutes

Procedure:

Gather the hikers together. Explain to them that they will have an opportunity to be quiet in nature, to pay attention to what they are experiencing, and to notice all the life and sounds that abound in nature. Explain that you will be walking ahead along the path laying out cards. Give the following directions:

- Walk fifty feet behind the person in front of you.

- Don't talk to each other.

- Stop and read each card; do or think about what is on the card.

Walk ahead down a path and lay out the index cards that you have prepared in advance (see below). You should also bring blank cards that you can write out as you go along to teach about specific things you notice on the path, and a few that simply have an arrow to point out directions. You should have a total of about thirty cards ready for the hike.

Assign a person to dismiss walkers in about fifty-foot intervals. This person will walk last and should pick up the cards as he or she goes along the walk. The walk ends when everyone reaches the leader.

Card Ideas

- Look up. What do you see?

- If you were a bird, where would you build a nest?

- Can you find the letter *alef* in nature?

- Find two things that depend upon each other.

- Rabbi Joshua ben Levi said, "Why is Israel likened to an olive tree? To tell you that just as the olive tree does not lose its leaves either in summer or in winter, so Israel shall never be lost either in this world or in the world to come." (Menachot 53b)

- "As civilization advances, the sense of wonder declines. Such decline is an alarming symptom of our state of mind. We will not perish for want of information, but only for want of appreciation." (A.J. Heschel, *Man is Not Alone*)

- "All that we see—the heavens, the Earth, and all that fills it—all these things are the outer garments of God." (Shneur Zalman, Tanya 42)

- Take your shoes off and walk barefoot to the next card.

- Smell this leaf.

- Close your eyes and listen for three natural sounds.

- Pretend you are a rock. What would it be like to be here for years and years?

- Make up a name for this plant.

- Look for three flying things.

- Think of a friend back home. What would you tell him or her about this journey?

- Write one line of a nature poem. [Place a journal or paper and a pen or pencil with this card.]

- Put your hands on the ground and make a wish for the earth.

- "The earth is the Eternal's and all that it holds...." (Psalm 24:1)

- Close your eyes and explore the bark of this tree.

- In your own way, take a moment to thank God for the gift of living.

- How can you tell that God is in this place?

- "We thank You...for your miracles that are with us each day, and for your wonders and your goodness at every moment: evening, morning, and noon." (daily Shaharit service)

- "To everything there is a season.... A time to be born, and a time to die." (Ecclesiastes 3:1–2)

Ending variations:

- At the end of the hike, the leader may want to put a card down that asks each hiker to take a pencil and pad to write a nature poem or prayer.

- At the end of the hike, have people sit alone quietly.

Card variation: Choose a theme for the hike and write cards designed for that theme.

Questions to Ask Hikers:

- What was your experience on the walk?

- Did you see anything unexpected?

- What was your favorite card? What did you like about it?

- How do you think the verse "while you walk on your way" is connected to this hike?

- Will you feel differently about the Ve'ahavta the next time you recite it?

- Would your experience on this stretch of trail have been different if you had walked together as a group and not followed any cards? How?

- If you were to make up your own cards, what would you write on them?

Perek Shirah: The Psalms of Life

he Bible teaches us that every plant and animal sings a song of praise to God. Psalm 148 urges "fruitful trees and all cedars, wild animals and all cattle, creeping things and winged birds, kings of the earth and all peoples" (9–11) to praise God. The hasidic leader Rabbi Nahman of Bratslav (1771–1811) taught that every part of nature has its own melody. And in Psalm 19, it is written that when we see the world with spiritually open eyes, we may see that "the heavens declare the glory of God, and the sky proclaims God's handiwork."

The *siddur* at one time actually included a section called "Perek Shirah," which spelled out the lyrics to the songs that each creature sang. As we spend more time in nature and listen carefully with our imaginations, perhaps we can hear the songs of praise sung by the works of creation around us.

Ages: 13+

Hikers' Goals:

- to appreciate other parts of creation as being alive and connected to God

- to experience the beauty of the psalms and the nature imagery contained in them

Materials:

- a pad and pen for each hiker

- a translation of Psalm 148

Procedure:

Read Psalm 148 to introduce the idea that all creation sings praises to God.

Psalm 148

Hallelujah. Praise Adonai from the heavens, praise God on high. Praise God, all the angels, praise God, all the hosts. Praise God, sun and moon, all shining stars. Praise God, highest heavens, and the waters that are above the heavens. Let them all praise the glory of Adonai, at whose command they were created, at whose decree they endure forever, and by whose laws nature abides. Praise Adonai, all who share the earth: all sea monsters and ocean depths, fire and hail, snow and smoke, storms that obey God's command; all mountains and hills, all fruit trees and cedars, all wild and tame beasts, creeping creatures, winged birds; earthly rulers, all the nations, officers and judges, men and women, young and old. Let all praise the glory of Adonai, for God alone is sublime, more magnificent than the earth and the heavens. God's glory encompasses heaven and earth. God exalts and extols the faithful, the people Israel who are close to God. Hallelujah.

Introduce the following creative writing exercise: Imagine what it would be like to be some part of creation other than a human being. What would your life be like? What might you see or feel? What would be your song of life? What would you praise God for?

Designate an area and allow hikers five minutes to walk around and choose a living creature or a feature of the landscape or weather that is of interest to them. Have them study it closely and stay by it. Allow fifteen minutes for them to write a song of praise on its behalf.

Invite hikers to share their songs of praise in any manner they choose, including simply reading the songs.

After all the hikers have shared their songs of praise, have them look around and try to hear the chorus of all things around them singing their songs simultaneously.

Questions to Ask Hikers:

• Is it hard to imagine that some things in nature would sing a song of praise to God?

• How would your behavior change if you recognized that everything in the world has a relationship with God?

Prayers, Poems, and Our Neshamot

abbi Nahman of Bratslav, one of the great hasidic masters, instructed his disciples to go outdoors daily and pray. Nature appreciation was not an end in itself to Rabbi Nahman; rather, he saw nature as a place to nourish one's *neshama* (soul) and encounter God. Our tradition is filled with beautiful poems and prayers about nature. In this activity hikers will have the chance to read some, as well as to write their own.

Ages: 13+

Hikers' Goals:

• to become familiar with poems about nature from Jewish tradition

• to write a poem about nature

Materials:

• journals or paper and writing utensils

Procedure: Read the following text:

"In order to serve God, one needs access to the enjoyment of the beauties of nature, such as the contemplation of flower-decorated meadows, majestic mountains, and flowing rivers. For all these are essential to the spiritual development of even the holiest of people."

—*Ha-Mispik La-Avodat ha-Shem*
RABBI ABRAHAM BEN MOSES BEN MAIMON (1186–1237)

Discuss the text and explain how religious masters used nature as a way to nourish their neshamot and as a means to reach God.

Distribute copies of "Prayers and Poems about Nature" and writing material. Have hikers find their own spots to read the prayers. Invite them to write their own prayer, poem, or piece of nature wisdom. This should take fifteen to thirty minutes. Regroup and share.

Variations: Hikers go in *ḥevruta* pairs and read the prayers together. After discussing the prayers they separate and write on their own.

Prayers and Poems about Nature:

It is special to go out into the fields at the start of spring,
When nature awakens from her sleep,
And to pour out a prayer there.
For every fresh blade of grass, every new flower,
All join themselves with prayer,
For they too yearn and long for God.

—*Maggid Sichot*
RABBI NAHMAN OF BRATSLAV

Master of the universe
grant me the ability to be alone;
May it be my custom to go outdoors each day
among the reeds and the grass,
among all growing things;
And there may I be alone
to enter into prayer,
talking to the ONE to whom I belong.

May I express there everything in my heart,
and may all the foliage of the field awake at my coming,
To send the powers of their life
into the words of my prayer,
So that my speech is made whole
through the life and spirit of all growing things,
Which are made as ONE by their Transcendent Source.

—RABBI NAHMAN OF BRATSLAV
(TRANSLATION BY RABBI SHAMAI KANTER)

The best remedy for those who are afraid, lonely, or unhappy is to go out-
side, somewhere where they can be quite alone with the heavens, nature
and God. Because only then does one feel that all is as it should be and
that God wishes to see people happy, amidst the simple beauty
of nature. As long as this exists, and it certainly always will,
I know that then there will always be comfort for every sorrow....
And I firmly believe that nature brings solace in all troubles.

—*Diary of a Young Girl*
ANNE FRANK

Questions to Ask Hikers:

- Whom or what did you appreciate during the time you were given the opportunity to stop and observe nature?

- How does reading Jewish prayers or poems about nature change your view of Judaism? Of nature?

- Do you think being in nature makes one more receptive to God?

Rabbi Meir Blessings Walk

ewish tradition contains blessings for seeing rainbows and hearing thunder, for eating food and excreting waste, for smelling flowers and sighting the first buds of spring, and for witnessing sites of extreme ugliness or beauty. The opportunities for reciting blessings are constant; one must therefore be constantly alert. In fact, second-century sage Rabbi Meir expected Jews to recite as many as one hundred blessings per day. Imagine how awake to the world we would have to be in order to say one hundred different meaningful blessings each day!

Ages: 9+

Hikers' Goals:

- to offer blessings in response to sensory experiences

- to become alert to and aware of one's surroundings

- to experience team work

Materials:

- cards with *birchot hanehenin* blessings (one blessing per card—in Hebrew, transliteration, and translation—and what it is meant to bless); at least two cards for each blessing, depending on size of group

Procedure:

Introduce hikers to the *birchot hanehenin* blessings—traditional blessings recited in response to sensory experiences (see below), most of which are connected to the natural world.

Ask the hikers if they normally make blessings in their lives. Discuss what they find meaningful and what they find difficult about the concept of reciting blessings. Discuss how blessings can foster awareness of the natural world and express gratitude and wonder.

Pass out one blessing card to each hiker. Instruct the hikers, quietly, by themselves, to go out into the surrounding area and find something that fulfills the blessing on the card they have been handed, and to recite that blessing. They should try to be fully "awake and present" to what is around them and to recite their designated blessings in response to sensory experiences.

When they have done this, they should return to the leader. The hikers should then find others who received cards with the same blessing. All those with the same blessings should then take up to ten minutes to make up a skit, song, poem, or cheer for their blessing, so that the other hikers will know what they have just blessed.

For example, the *shekachah lo ba'olamo* group might plan and perform a cheer for seeing something magnificent, such as:
"A beautiful bud!
A silver lake!
A lovely rock!
A little snake!
Thanks, God, for a magnificent world!"
The presenters then let the others guess which blessing they went out to recite.

Questions to Ask Hikers:

- Was it easy to find the thing you were assigned to bless?
- Do you think God appreciates our blessings?
- Does the flower, tree, animal, etc. being blessed appreciate our blessings?
- Does saying a blessing change us?
- Will you remember your assigned blessing? Why?

Birchot Hanehenin:

On experiencing shooting stars, earthquakes, lightning, thunder, and storms:

בָּרוּךְ אַתָּה, יְיָ אֱלֹהֵינוּ, מֶלֶךְ הָעוֹלָם, שֶׁכֹּחוֹ וּגְבוּרָתוֹ מָלֵא עוֹלָם.

Baruch atah, Adonai Eloheinu, Melech ha'olam, she'koho ug'vurato malei olam.

Blessed are You, Adonai our God, Ruler of the universe, whose power and might fill the entire world.

On seeing natural wonders—mountains, valleys, oceans, rivers, and wilderness:

בָּרוּךְ אַתָּה, יְיָ אֱלֹהֵינוּ, מֶלֶךְ הָעוֹלָם, עֹשֶׂה מַעֲשֵׂה בְרֵאשִׁית.

Baruch atah, Adonai Eloheinu, Melech ha'olam, oseh ma'asei v'reishit.

Blessed are You, Adonai our God, Ruler of the universe, who makes the wonders of creation.

On seeing trees in blossom for the first time in a season:

בָּרוּךְ אַתָּה, יְיָ אֱלֹהֵינוּ, מֶלֶךְ הָעוֹלָם, שֶׁלֹּא חִסַּר בְּעוֹלָמוֹ דָּבָר,
וּבָרָא בוֹ בְּרִיּוֹת טוֹבוֹת וְאִילָנוֹת טוֹבִים לְהַנּוֹת בָּהֶם בְּנֵי אָדָם.

*Baruch atah, Adonai Eloheinu, Melech ha'olam, shelo hisar b'olam davar
uvarah vo briyot tovot v'ilanot tovim l'hanot bahem b'nei adam.*

Blessed are You, Adonai our God, Ruler of the universe, who has
withheld nothing from the world and who has created beautiful
creatures and beautiful trees for humans to enjoy.

On seeing rainbows:

בָּרוּךְ אַתָּה, יְיָ אֱלֹהֵינוּ, מֶלֶךְ הָעוֹלָם, זוֹכֵר הַבְּרִית וְנֶאֱמָן בִּבְרִיתוֹ
וְקַיָּם בְּמַאֲמָרוֹ.

*Baruch atah, Adonai Eloheinu, Melech ha'olam, zocher habrit v'ne'eman
bivrito v'kayam b'ma'amaro.*

Praised are You, Adonai our God, Ruler of the universe, who
remembers the covenant, is faithful to it, and keeps God's
promise.

Over rain and over good news:

בָּרוּךְ אַתָּה, יְיָ אֱלֹהֵינוּ, מֶלֶךְ הָעוֹלָם, הַטּוֹב וְהַמֵּטִיב.

Baruch atah, Adonai Eloheinu, Melech ha'olam, hatov v'hameitiv.

Blessed are You, Adonai our God, Ruler of the universe, who is
good and does goodness.

On seeing something magnificent:

בָּרוּךְ אַתָּה, יְיָ אֱלֹהֵינוּ, מֶלֶךְ הָעוֹלָם, שֶׁכָּכָה לוֹ בָּעוֹלָמוֹ.

Baruch atah, Adonai Eloheinu, Melech ha'olam, shekachah lo ba'olamo.

Blessed are You, Adonai our God, Ruler of the universe, who has things such as this in God's world.

On smelling dried herbs or spices:

בָּרוּךְ אַתָּה, יְיָ אֱלֹהֵינוּ, מֶלֶךְ הָעוֹלָם, בּוֹרֵא מִינֵי בְשָׂמִים.

Baruch atah, Adonai Eloheinu, Melech ha'olam, borei minei v'samim.

Blessed are You, Adonai our God, Ruler of the universe, who creates various spices.

On smelling the fragrance of grasses or plants:

בָּרוּךְ אַתָּה, יְיָ אֱלֹהֵינוּ, מֶלֶךְ הָעוֹלָם, בּוֹרֵא עִשְׂבֵי בְשָׂמִים.

Baruch atah, Adonai Eloheinu, Melech ha'olam, borei isvei v'samim.

Blessed are You, Adonai our God, Ruler of the universe, who creates fragrant plants.

Before eating fruit:

בָּרוּךְ אַתָּה, יְיָ אֱלֹהֵינוּ, מֶלֶךְ הָעוֹלָם, בּוֹרֵא פְּרִי הָעֵץ.

Baruch atah, Adonai Eloheinu, Melech ha'olam, borei pri ha'etz.

Blessed are You, Adonai our God, Ruler of the universe, who creates the fruit of the tree.

Questions to Ask Hikers:

- How many things were you able to notice and experience? Were you surprised by the amount?

- What was it like to say a blessing for almost everything you experienced?

- Do you think God appreciates our blessings? What about the flower, animal, and so on, over which the blessing is said?

- Does saying blessings change us?

- What would you be like if you said blessings more often?

- What is another way you can experience wonder and gratitude if you do not feel comfortable reciting blessings to God?

Mikveh Renewal

A mikveh is a Jewish ritual bath traditionally used for spiritual purification (such as conversion to Judaism) and before holidays and special occasions. The *mikveh* ritual requires a person to immerse one's entire body in a source of "living water," that is, water collected naturally (e.g., rainwater, or water from a spring, lake, sea, or certain rivers). It is wonderful to do a *mikveh* ritual outdoors. The purpose of this activity is not to fulfill the *mitzvah* of immersion, but rather to take part in a *mikveh* ritual of personal renewal and rebirth.

Hikers' Goals:

- to learn about the ritual of *mikveh*
- to experience personal renewal and growth
- to appreciate natural water sources

Location: a location with natural water

Materials:

- towels
- bathing suits (Optional—traditionally, immersion in a *mikveh* requires undressing. However, hikers may wear bathing suits as comfort or policy dictates. In either case, *mikveh* rituals provide a wonderful opportunity for separate men's and women's experiences.)

Procedure:

Find a spot in the water that is deep enough for hikers to immerse themselves completely but that is safe from overly turbulent water and other hazards and is accessible to rescue. Define boundaries and guidelines for hikers. A certified lifeguard should be present during this activity.

There are many ways to perform the *mikveh* ritual. Here is one suggestion:

Invite the hikers to reflect upon what this *mikveh* means to them. Specifically, what would they like to cleanse themselves of, and what would they like to bring to themselves? This *kavanah* (intention/hope) can be kept private or shared with the group.

If you are in a public place, you may want to post one person at the trail head as a *shomer* (guard) to ensure the group's privacy. This can help hikers focus on their ritual. Make sure everyone is monitored while in the water.

Hikers should enter the *mikveh* one at a time. Just before entering the water is a good time to share one's *kavanah*. Once in the water, hikers should completely immerse themselves three times. The *mikveh* blessing can be recited after the first immersion.

Singing or chanting before, during, and after the *mikveh* ritual can help create a reflective, celebratory mood. Conclude by reciting the following blessing:

בָּרוּךְ אַתָּה, יְיָ אֱלֹהֵינוּ, מֶלֶךְ הָעוֹלָם, אֲשֶׁר קִדְּשָׁנוּ בְּמִצְוֹתָיו וְצִוָּנוּ עַל הַטְּבִילָה.

Baruch atah, Adonai Eloheinu, Melech ha'olam, asher kidshanu b'mitzvotav v'tzivanu al hatevilah.

Blessed are You, Adonai our God, Ruler of the universe, who sanctified us with the commandments and commanded us regarding immersion.

Debriefing:

The group's reuniting, after the hikers have shared a profound experience while divided according to sex, is a time for sensitivity. In bringing the group together, respect the privacy and specialness of the intimate time that the participants spent by themselves. The leader may ask each group to share highlights of their *mikveh* rituals.

CHAPTER 6

Ma'ariv Aravim: Blessing the Night

N ight is often associated with fear. Evil spirits and demons were once thought to make their rounds after the sun set. Our fear of night has a biological basis as well. We humans depend upon our eyes for approximately 80 percent of our sensory input from the outside world. In the darkness, as our eyesight diminishes, so does our ability to comprehend the world. As our comprehension diminishes, our fear increases.

Judaism recognizes that night can be a scary time. Hashkivenu, a traditional prayer in the evening service, asks God to protect us. Yet Judaism also recognizes that night is as much a part of God's creation as day. In the evening prayers, before the Sh'ma, Jews praise God, *ma'ariv aravim*, "who brings on evenings."

Night was often the time when our ancestors and prophets felt God's presence. Jacob's wrestling match with a divine being took place in the dark of night. Often God would become known to prophets during their nighttime dreams.

The night can be a special time to be in the wilderness. Stars, nocturnal animals, and the cool of the night on one's skin cannot be experienced during the day. The activities in this section are designed to make participants comfortable in the dark and to convey the sacred quality of the nighttime experience.

Bringing On the Night

Night is often mysterious and scary for humans because our eyesight is greatly diminished. Yet, in truth, our eyes do function well in the dark. Going on a night hike without the use of flashlights can be an exhilarating experience. Flashlights tend to ruin the night mood and prevent hikers from developing a trust in their night vision. Unless you are in a dense forest during the new moon, when there is no moonlight, it is not difficult to make your way relying on the ambient light of the moon and the stars.

Ages: 10+

Hikers' Goals:

- to eliminate fear of the night
- to appreciate the darkness of the night

Materials:

- candles and matches
- blindfolds
- six similar items but of different colors (felt-tip markers work well)
- sheet of paper
- flashlight (for emergency use by the leader)

Procedure:

This activity actually comprises four activities that, if done together, make up a one-hour night hike. To begin, ask the hikers how they feel about being out in the night. Read Ma'ariv Aravim, and compare the tone of the prayer to hikers' feelings. (You may find that hikers have a fear of night. Compare this to Ma'ariv Aravim, where God is blessed for bringing on the night.)

Ma'ariv Aravim Prayer

Blessed are You, Adonai, Ruler of the universe, who, with your word, brings on evenings. With wisdom God opens the gates and with understanding changes the times and alternates the seasons and arranges the stars in their watches, in the sky, according to God's will. God creates day and night. God rolls light away from before darkness and darkness from before light. God causes day to pass and brings night and separates between day and night. Adonai is God's name. The Almighty, alive and enduring, will always reign over us. Blessed are You, Adonai, who brings on the evening.

Caterpillar Walk

Have the hikers stand in single file with their hands on the shoulders of the person in front of them. Instruct them to close their eyes and be silent. The hands of the first person in line go on the shoulders of the leader, who leads the line on a five- to ten-minute walk.

Questions to Ask Hikers:

- How did you feel as you walked? How did you feel afterward?

- Did you have more trust in your feet as the walk progressed?

- What happened to your other senses on this walk?

- How did the night feel on your skin?

- What did you like about being out in the night?

Bat and Moth

Have the hikers stand in a circle; pick two people to stand in the middle. Explain that bats are effective nighttime hunters. They hunt their prey using not only their sight but also their "echo-location" ability. They make a high-pitched sound that bounces off moths and other small animals, enabling the bats to locate their prey.

Blindfold one hiker, who will be the bat. Instruct the bat to make a noise like "bop." Another person is designated the moth. Every time the bat says "bop," the moth must respond with "beep."

The object of the game is for the bat to find the moth. The hikers who make up the circumference of the circle act as a safety net to prevent the bat and moth from leaving the circle. (If the moth is too difficult to catch, decrease the size of the circle.)

Questions to Ask Hikers:

• What strategies did the successful bats employ?

• What strategies did the successful moths employ?

• What other animals depend on hearing to catch their prey?

Day and Night Vision

This activity should be done in a dark area. Have the hikers sit in a circle, and place the six colored objects inside the circle. Pick up each object, one at a time, and pass it around the circle, having hikers guess the color of the object. Once all objects have been passed around and returned to their original places, instruct the hikers to cover one eye, their "night-vision eye." Light the candle and show the hikers the colors of the objects in the light of the candle.

With their night-vision eye remaining covered, the hikers should then look at the candle with their uncovered "day-vision eye." Blow out the candle and have the hikers look at one another with their day-vision eye. Then ask them to cover their day-vision eye, uncover their night-vision eye and look at each other. They should notice that the night-vision eye can see much better. Explain that humans really do possess good night vision, but that we scarcely use it in our urban and suburban lifestyles.

Creating a Group Prayer

The hike began with reading Ma'ariv Aravim. It can end with a group prayer or poem, when you return to a well-lit place.

Take a sheet of paper and have one hiker write the first line of a nighttime prayer. The hiker passes the sheet to the next hiker, who reads the first line and adds a second. Before passing the sheet to the next hiker, the second folds the sheet so the first line is covered. The third hiker, who can read only the second line that was written, writes a third line and then folds the sheet so only that line is visible. The sheet is then passed on; continue like this until everyone writes a line of the prayer.

Read the prayer aloud.

Kiddush Levanah: Moon Blessings

According to Jewish tradition, between the seventh and the thirteenth day of the Jewish month, we are to go outside on a clear night and perform the *kiddush levanah* ceremony while viewing the waxing moon. *kiddush levanah* is the only Jewish ritual in which we are commanded to go outside and encounter an element of the natural world solely for our spiritual benefit. In fact, Rabbi Yohanan stated that "one who greets the moon at its proper time, it is as if he greets the *Shechinah* (divine presence)."

The cycles of the moon, as it waxes and wanes, can be seen as a metaphor for the spiritual evolution of an individual or of the nation of Israel. We all go through alternating periods of nothingness or darkness—a feeling of death in some way—and of increasing light, or clarity, and power.

In the *kiddush levanah* ceremony, the waxing moon is celebrated as a symbol of increasing light—the return to power. It is designed to help us tap into our power of renewal by bringing light and an awareness of God into our own lives. The activities that follow expand upon the themes that are presented in the traditional *kiddush levanah* service.

Ages: 13+

Hikers' Goals:

• to experience the waxing moon as an inspiration for personal renewal

• to participate in a *kiddush levanah* ceremony

Procedure:

Find a place where the hikers have a clear view of the moon and adequate space to move and interact. (On extended hikes, share with the group the anticipation of looking for the moon and waiting for a clear night.)

Before starting the service, help hikers focus by having them explore their senses. Ask them, "What do you hear? What do you smell? What sensations do you feel on your skin? in your body?" Then invite hikers to focus on the new moon.

Briefly explain the cycles of the moon as it progresses from invisibility to fullness and then back again, and how these cycles symbolize the spiritual experience of each of us and Israel as a nation. Explain that the *kiddush levanah* ceremony is designed to help us tap into our power of renewal and to bring light into our lives. This ceremony also works well if you just jump right into it, without first intellectualizing the experience.

Recite a few lines from the traditional service:

"Hallelujah! Praise God from the heavens, praise God from the heights. Praise God all God's servants...praise God sun and moon. Praise God all stars of light...."

"And to the moon [God] said that she should be renewed, a crown of glory to those born of the womb, who will renew themselves like her.... Blessed are You, who renews the months."

Address the moon, saying: "Blessed is your Designer, blessed is your Maker, blessed is your Owner, blessed is your Creator."

Do at least one of the following activities to ritualize personal renewal:

Read the introduction to this activity, and then give hikers two to three minutes to sit and appreciate the moonlight and the concept of rebirth and renewal. Then hike peacefully, without saying anything. This step helps the hikers to validate their experiences without any verbalizing or intellectualizing.

Invite the hikers to imagine the light of the moon entering into some part of themselves that they wish to reenergize at this time, and to express this vision through movement. The traditional *kiddush levanah* service includes instructions for worshipers to look at the moon and to rise up on one's toes, as if in dance. Have the hikers start and/or end their movements in such a posture: on their toes, reaching toward the moon.

Invite pairs of hikers to share affirmations in which they fill in the blanks in the sentences. For example: I'm letting go of _____. I'm giving birth to _____ in myself. I'm letting light in to _____. I welcome in _____.

Conclude in traditional fashion, by wishing one another peace:

Shalom aleichem. May peace be unto you.
Aleichem shalom. Unto you may there be peace.

Questions to Ask Hikers:

- Did you feel comfortable taking the moon into some part of yourself?

- Why did Rabbi Yoḥanan say, "One who greets the moon at its proper time, it is as if he greets the *Shechinah*"?

Jacob's Night Struggle

ne night, while on a journey, our ancestor Jacob sent his family, his companions, and all his possessions across a *wadi* (ravine). The Torah tells us that "Jacob was left alone, and there wrestled a man with him until the breaking of the day." (Genesis 32:25) Some commentators believe this unidentified man was an angel. Others say Jacob was wrestling with himself, with his own conscience and fears. In any case, when dawn arose, Jacob received a blessing: a new name, Israel, meaning one who struggles with God.

It is no coincidence that Jacob's struggle took place when he was alone, at night. Nighttime darkness sparks one's imagination, and when one is left alone in the night, fears and vulnerabilities can come to the surface. This activity is designed to give hikers a taste of what that night must have been like for Jacob— a chance to confront their own fears and earn the name Israel for themselves.

Ages: 13+

Hikers' Goals:

• to identify with Jacob's struggle

• to acknowledge and confront fears and vulnerability, while building comfort with the nighttime and darkness

Procedure:

Tell or study together the story of Jacob's struggle (Genesis 32:4–29). Introduce the idea of sitting alone at night in a way that will simulate Jacob's experience. Explain that it is perfectly normal for one to become afraid while sitting alone in the dark. This, in fact, is the point of the exercise—to learn about oneself by identifying such fears and grappling with them. When fears arise, encourage hikers to meet the "angel" that carries them.

Where does this angel come from? What does the angel need to leave them in peace? Try to confront the angel/fear, and ask for its blessing instead.

In a level spot on the trail without hazards (water, poisonous plants, and so on), invite hikers to take ten to twenty steps off the trail in any direction and then to stay put in that spot. The limit is crucial for safety and for hikers to stay within hearing distance. Tell them how much time they will have alone. They should spread out sufficiently for each person to feel somewhat alone and to be unable to see others. This activity should take place in silence.

After the specified interval, call the hikers back to the trail. Use a sound rather than words (e.g., an animal call or a song) and continue calling so the hikers can follow the sound back to the trail.

Important note: As with any activity that involves emotional risk-taking, the leader must be sensitive to hikers who have experienced trauma and who may encounter a high level of anxiety during this activity; pair them up if necessary. It is crucial that participation in this activity be voluntary.

Questions to Ask Hikers:

- What was it like to be alone in the night?

- What were you afraid of? Did you imagine you saw or heard anything that wasn't there?

- Did you gain any insight into this fear? Were you able to confront it? to change its message from one of fear to one of blessing? (Remind hikers that the struggle itself is valuable—after all, Jacob left his struggle limping.)

- Did you become more comfortable in the darkness as your time alone continued?

Life of a Star

annah Senesh was a Hungarian/Israeli poet who fought as a partisan during World War II. She parachuted into Nazi-controlled Europe, where she was captured and executed by the Nazis.

She wrote the following:

"There are stars whose radiance is visible on earth though they have long been extinct. There are people whose brilliance continues to light the world though they are no longer among the living. These lights are particularly bright when the night is dark. They light the way for humankind."

Ages: 12+

Hikers' Goals:

- to recognize how Hannah Senesh's poetry reflects the life of a star

Materials:

- flashlight
- an eight-by-ten-inch piece of cardboard with glow-in-the-dark stars set in the form of the Big Dipper constellation

Procedure:

Take the group to a place where everyone can see the night sky with minimal light interference. Ask hikers what they think of when they look at the stars. Shine the flashlight on the cardboard until the stars glow. Help the hikers locate the Big Dipper in the sky by showing them the glowing stars on the cardboard. While your group is looking at these stars, tell them the following story about the life of a star:

A star is a ball of gas and dust that is in a constant state of nuclear fusion—hydrogen gas turning into helium. Tremendous amounts of energy are released in this process and create the light we see when we look at a star. When the gas burns out, the star burns out.

Our sun is a star and is estimated to be about halfway through its life span. That means it has another 5 to 10 billion years of fusion left. We on Earth experience the energy released from our sun in the form of light and heat.

Astronomers do not know exactly how a star's life progresses because its life span is so much longer than ours, but they think that a star is born when gases are pulled together by gravitational forces and fusion begins. It burns hydrogen for billions of years until most of its gas burns out.

Because the distance between Earth and the stars is so vast, we measure it in light years. A light year is the distance light covers while traveling at 186,000 miles per second for a year—about 6 trillion miles. It is conceivable that we see the light from a star that has already burned out if the star is many light years away. For example, the star Arcturus is forty light years away, which means that the light we see from it today left the star about forty years ago.

Explain who Hannah Senesh was and read the selection from "Blessed Is the Match." She knew that stars eventually burn out, but that their light continues to be seen; her poem likens this to the impact of some human beings whose presence is felt for years after their death. Hannah Senesh is such a star.

Questions to Ask Hikers:

• What are your impressions of Hannah Senesh's poem?

• Can you think of anyone in history or in your life whose light still burns for you?

Values Index